COUNTRIES OF THE WORLD

UNITED KINGDOM

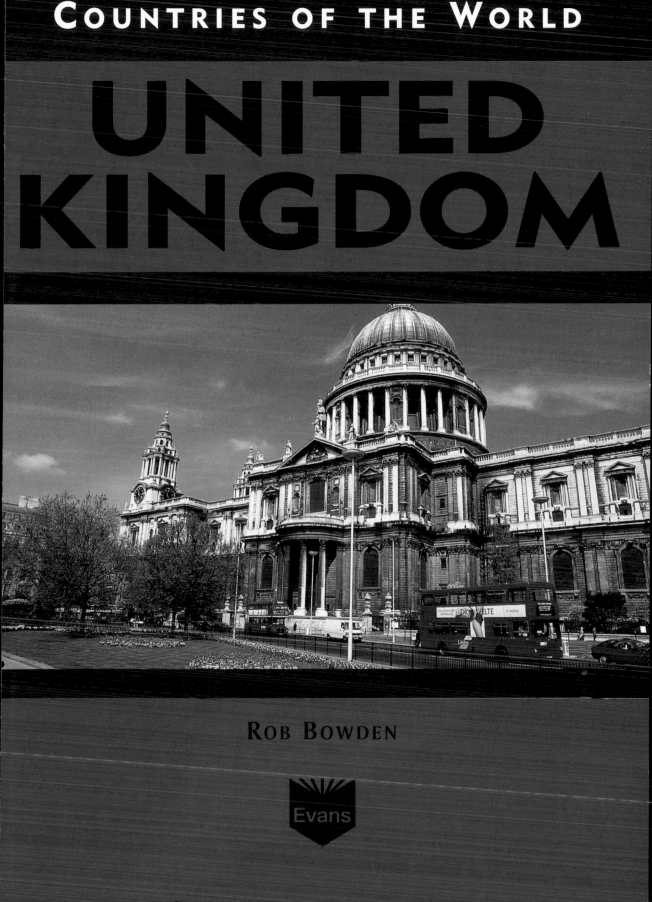

ROB BOWDEN

Evans

TITLES IN THE COUNTRIES OF THE WORLD SERIES:

ARGENTINA • AUSTRALIA • BRAZIL • CANADA • CHINA
EGYPT • FRANCE • GERMANY • INDIA • ITALY • JAPAN
KENYA • MEXICO • NIGERIA • POLAND • UNITED KINGDOM
USA • VIETNAM

Published by Evans Brothers Limited
2A Portman Mansions
Chiltern Street
London W1U 6NR

VISIT OUR WEBSITE
www.evansbooks.co.uk

Reprinted with revisions 2005

Produced for Evans Brothers Limited by
Monkey Puzzle Media Limited
Gissing's Farm, Fressingfield
Suffolk IP21 5SH

First published 2002
© copyright Evans Brothers 2002

British Library Cataloguing in Publication Data
United Kingdom. - (Countries of the world)
1.Great Britain - Juvenile literature
I.Title
941

ISBN 0 237 52802 9

Editor: Katie Orchard
Designer: Jane Hawkins
Map artwork by Peter Bull
Charts and graphs produced by Encompass Graphics Ltd

Endpapers (front): The stunning landscape of
the Scottish Highlands.
Title page: St Paul's Cathedral – a key feature
of the London skyline.
Imprint and Contents page: The mysterious
structures of Stonehenge date back 5,000 years.
Endpapers (back): The Queen's Guards march
down Pall Mall towards Buckingham Palace.

All photografhs taken by Rob Bowden (images@easi-er.co.uk) except for the following, which were kindly supplied by: *Chapel Studios* front
endpapers (Graham Horner), title page (Patrick Cockell), 11 (top/Zul Mukhida), 11 (bottom/David Thomas), 12 (Graham Horner), 14
(top/Graham Horner), 14–15 (bottom/Zul Mukhida), 16 (bottom/Zul Mukhida), 20 (top and bottom/Graham Horner), 21 (top/Zul Mukhida), 23
(Graham Horner), 25 (top/Graham Horner), 28 (Zul Mukhida), 35 (bottom/Graham Horner), 37 (Zul Mukhida), 42 (Graham Horner), 44
(top/Graham Horner), 45 (Rafe Harwood), 46 (top/Tim Garrod), 48 (Graham Horner), 57 (top and bottom/Zul Mukhida); *Corbis* 60 (Grant
Smith); *Corbis Digital Stock* imprint and contents pages, back endpapers; *FLPA* 38 (Chris Demetriou), 51 (J Watkins).

CONTENTS

The Union Flag, combining
the flags of England, Scotland
and Northern Ireland.

Liverpool's famous waterfront across the River Mersey. Liverpool was one of the many cities that benefited from trade during the colonial period.

A UNITED KINGDOM?

The UK is a political union between the island of Great Britain (made up of England, Scotland and Wales) and Northern Ireland. However, the union as it stands today was only formed in 1921, when the Anglo-Irish Treaty agreed to the partition, or division, of Ireland. The oldest part of the union is between England and Wales (1536). Scotland joined later to form Great Britain in 1707. A union between Great Britain and Ireland in 1801 led to the formation of the United Kingdom of Great Britain and Ireland, which survived until the 1921 Anglo-Irish Agreement. This agreement eventually led to the present union and name.

The UK's complicated past continues to present fresh challenges today. Scotland and Wales are arguing for greater independence, and there has been a long-standing struggle for power in Northern Ireland between those loyal to Ireland and those loyal to Great Britain.

There is often confusion about the use of the name 'UK': many people use the terms 'Great Britain' or even 'England' instead. This is perhaps understandable given that the capital, London, is in England and the national language is English.

RULE BRITANNIA

In its prime the UK controlled over a quarter of the earth's surface and ruled over almost half of the world's population. These were the days of the British Empire, which began with the colonisation of North America and the Caribbean in the early 1600s and peaked in the late 1800s before starting to decline after the First World War (1914–18). During this period the UK became the world's greatest trading and military nation, amassing great wealth from its colonies and territories around the world. This wealth helped fund the Industrial Revolution that began in Britain around 1760, nearly 40 years before the USA began to industrialise and 70 years before the rest of western Europe.

By the time of the First World War, however, the British Empire was starting to lose its world superiority. The USA and Germany had taken over as the primary industrial powers and political control was being challenged by colonies throughout the empire. The enormous loss of human life (1.2 million

Castles are a reminder of the power struggles before the creation of the union. This one, built in 1285, is at Harlech in Wales.

people) and the massive economic costs of fighting two wars in close succession left the UK crippled. After the end of the Second World War (1939–1945), the UK was unable and unwilling to maintain its empire. In 1947 India gained its independence and this set off a series of movements that saw most colonies secure independence in the following 30 years. Some of the last colonies to gain independence were Zimbabwe in 1980 and Hong Kong, which became part of China in 1997.

This monument in Ironbridge is dedicated to the thousands who died during the two world wars.

KEY DATA

Official Name:	United Kingdom of Great Britain and Northern Ireland (UK)
Area:	244,100km²
Population:	59,400,000 (2004 estimate)
Official Language:	English
Main Cities:	London (capital), Birmingham, Manchester, Edinburgh, Cardiff, Belfast
GDP per capita:	US$ 27,700 (2003 estimate)*
Currency:	Pound Sterling (£)
Exchange Rate:	US$1 = £0.55 (1 November 2004)

* Calculated on Purchasing Power Parity basis

Rebuilding the UK

After the loss of so many lives during the two world wars, the UK had to rebuild both its economy and its population. Rebuilding the economy was a slow process, but with financial assistance from the newly established international community (including organisations such as the United Nations and the World Bank) the UK economy was soon growing again. By 1957 Prime Minister Harold Macmillan famously stated that Britain 'had never had it so good'. Rebuilding the population, however, would take longer. The government created the Welfare State, setting up institutions such as the National Health Service (NHS) and providing free education to encourage and support families. This led to a baby boom in the population, but there were still not enough people of working age to help rebuild the economy in the short term. The UK turned to its colonies and encouraged people to come to the UK to live and work. Many thousands took up the invitation, with most arriving from India, Pakistan and the Caribbean, and settling in London and the big industrial cities of central England such as Birmingham, Sheffield and Manchester.

The arrival of these people not only aided economic recovery, but also made the UK into the multi-cultural society that it is today.

Manchester is one of many multi-ethnic cities in the UK.

By the 1960s the UK was again showing its strength with a booming economy and a thriving cultural scene that become known as 'the swinging sixties'. This period produced some of the UK's best-known symbols such as the Mini motor car, the music of *The Beatles* and *The Rolling Stones*, and the World Cup winning football champions of 1966.

The UK and Europe

In 1973 the UK joined the European Economic Community (now the European Union – EU) and so began a debate that is as current today as it was then – the relationship between the UK and Europe. Europe is vital to the UK economy, accounting for well over 50 per cent of all trade, but as other European countries introduce policies to further strengthen such ties, the UK has so far been reluctant to join them. The main argument surrounds the replacement of the UK currency with a common European currency (the Euro –   ). Many British people believe this would mean a further loss of independence and power for the UK economy. Others believe the UK must join the European Monetary Union (EMU) if it is to stay competitive with its European partners and that failure to do so could be disastrous for the UK economy.

TWENTY-FIRST CENTURY UK

The position of the UK at the beginning of the twenty-first century was very different from what it had been only a century before. No longer a world superpower, the UK is having to form new relationships with Europe and beyond in order to keep its position as a major world economy. At home it is also having to examine itself and the relationships between the different parts of the union. In 1997 the people of Scotland and Wales voted to have greater control over their own affairs in a process known as devolution. Northern Ireland, too, has a national assembly, but tension between the rival parties there constantly threaten its work.

With such diversity in the UK today, many people are now questioning what it means to be British. The early part of the twenty-first century is likely to see more changes to the nature of the UK.

ABOVE: Protestant Orangemen in Northern Ireland still celebrate the victory of William III over the Catholic forces of James II in 1690. BELOW: Edinburgh is the seat of the newly devolved Scottish parliament.

Dramatic hills tower over Scotland's stunning Loch Lomond.

The landscape of the UK is very varied, from the peaks of the Scottish Highlands to the low-lying areas of flat land in Norfolk that are no higher than sea level. Images of rolling hills are often associated with the UK, which has earned a reputation as a 'green and pleasant land', benefiting from fertile soil and a temperate climate. As an island nation, the UK's varied coastline is also an important aspect of the landscape.

THE HIGHLANDS

Scotland is the highest part of the UK, consisting of the North-west Highlands and Southern Uplands (bordering England) and the Grampian Mountains. There is a low-lying area in between where the main population centres (Edinburgh, Glasgow and Dundee) are found. The Highlands are carved up by numerous rivers and lochs (lakes). Loch Ness is world famous and has long been rumoured to be the home of a mysterious prehistoric creature. The western coastline is indented with steep-sided sea lochs and surrounded by most of Scotland's 790 islands, which include the Hebrides, Orkneys and Shetlands. People living on some of the 130 inhabited islands are amongst the most remote populations in the UK. Fierce seas and stormy weather often isolate these communities from the mainland for weeks at a time. Western Scotland's Grampians (including the Cairngorms) are the UK's highest range and include the UK's highest point, Ben Nevis, at 1,343m.

The Grampians are the only part of the UK high enough to support arctic vegetation. Wales is also dominated by highland and mountains, with the Cambrian Mountains running the length of the country. Better known, however, are the Brecon Beacons in the south-east and Snowdonia in the north-west. Snowdonia includes Mount Snowdon, Wales' highest peak at 1,085m. This is a popular tourist attraction, receiving over 500,000 visitors each year. Popular activities include walking or taking the train to the summit, complete with its own café!

THE LOWLANDS

The UK's lowlands are located mainly in England, particularly in the east of the country. In parts of Lincolnshire and East Anglia (Norfolk, Suffolk and Cambridgeshire) the land barely rises above sea level. Much of this area was once fertile wetlands known as 'the Fens'. In the eighteenth century the Fens were drained to create farmland that is today

ABOVE: A haunting mist rolls over Cader Idris, part of the spectacular mountain scenery of Snowdonia National Park in Wales.
RIGHT: Gently rolling hillsides dominate much of the UK and are extensively farmed, with sheep farming being the most widespread.

the main arable farming area of the UK with fields of grains or vegetables stretching as far as the eye can see. In the south-west, the Somerset Levels form another area of lowland which was drained for farming, but also for harvesting peat used as a fuel and, more recently, to enrich garden soils. During heavy rainfall this area often floods, returning the landscape to what it may have looked like several hundred years ago.

There is very little of the UK's landscape that has not been altered in some form by human activities. Originally much of the country would have been covered in woodland but most of this has now disappeared with only a few areas surviving such as the New Forest, near Southampton, and Sherwood Forest (made famous in the tales of Robin Hood), near Nottingham.

ROLLING HILLS

Between the extremes of the highlands and lowlands, the rest of the UK consists of gently rolling countryside. This land is generally well watered and fertile. Most of the UK population lives in this area and many of the main population centres are located near the country's major rivers such as London on the Thames, Nottingham on the Trent and Newcastle on the Tyne. Farming in this region is a mixture of arable and livestock with some regional specialisms. For example, dairy production is significant in the south-west – Devon cream is world famous.

LANDSCAPE OF THE UK

Rock climbers at Brimham Rocks, near Harrowgate in Yorkshire, make the most of the dramatic landscape.

Landscapes are important for tourism, too, and many of the most popular attractions are located in the UK's countryside areas. The Lake District in Cumbria is perhaps the best known, but other popular landscapes include the Pennines, the Peak District, the Yorkshire Moors, the Cotswolds, Dartmoor, Exmoor and the South Downs, all of which attract millions of visitors every year.

COASTAL LANDSCAPES

The UK is surrounded by water and has a coastline stretching a total of 12,429km – equivalent to travelling almost a third of the way around the world. This coastline varies dramatically from the pebbly beaches and chalk cliffs of Sussex to the expansive sands of north Norfolk, and the sheer cliffs and lochs of Scotland's west coast. One of the most popular coastal regions is south-west England, where the mixture of rugged granite cliffs, white sand beaches and picturesque fishing villages attract tourists in their millions. Some of the UK's best-loved towns are also on the coast, such as Brighton with its famous pier and Blackpool with its pleasure beach. These have become highly developed tourist centres for both foreign and UK visitors. One of the UK's more unusual coastal features is the world famous Giant's Causeway in County Antrim, Northern Ireland. This 5km-long stretch of basalt columns was formed by molten lava erupting from beneath the sea and cooling very quickly. The columns, which are hexagonal in shape, are between 37–50cm wide and vary in height up to 6m tall. From the air the Giant's Causeway looks like a giant honeycomb.

UNPREDICTABLE WEATHER

British people are famous for their discussions about the weather. When it rains they long for sunshine and yet after just a few weeks of dry, sunny weather they start to complain that their gardens are drying out and that it is too hot. In reality the UK's climate is usually somewhere in between these extremes and is classified as maritime temperate. This means it is generally mild and damp – rarely too hot and dry or too cold and wet.

British people are quick to enjoy the summer sunshine whilst it lasts!

The UK's weather is difficult to predict and can change very rapidly in a single day. Some general patterns can be identified, however. Temperatures tend to be warmer in the south than in the north. Average temperatures in the south of England range from 4°C in January to 18°C in July, whilst in the north of Scotland the averages range from 3°C to 15°C during the same months. Rainfall is higher in the west of the UK and on higher ground. The Scottish Highlands receive over 3,000mm per year, and in parts of the Pennines and the Lake District rainfall of up to 4,500mm has been recorded. Eastern and low-lying areas of the UK are generally drier, averaging around 1,000–1,500mm, but falling as low as 600mm in London and parts of neighbouring Kent and Essex.

The white chalk cliffs dominate the view at the Seven Sisters Country Park in Sussex.

TEMPERATURE AND RAINFALL

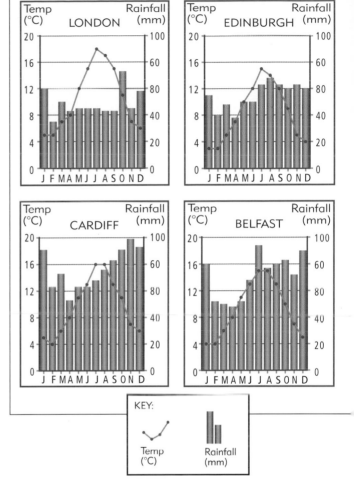

KEY:

Temp (°C)

Rainfall (mm)

CASE STUDY
STORMS AHOY!

In October 2000 and again in March 2001 parts of the UK experienced exceptional rainfall leading to serious flooding with damage to property and massive disruption to travel and daily life. In Lewes, in south-east England, 800 homes and businesses and over 700 cars were damaged or written-off by the floods. Rainfall in the area was more than three times its normal level during October 2000, yet by June 2001 rainfall was four times less than normal, causing localised drought in the same area. Such extremes are expected to become more common in future as a result of climate change and records suggest that this is already happening – 2001 saw the wettest March in the UK since 1766.

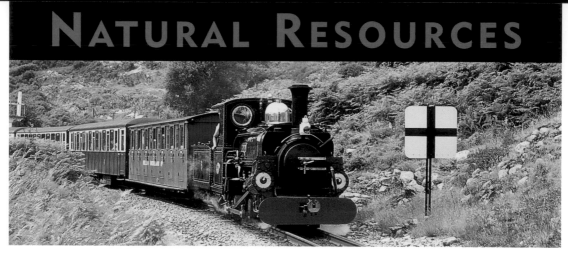

This old slate train in north Wales now provides scenic tourist rides.

RESOURCES FOR INDUSTRIALISATION

Although the UK does not have abundant supplies of natural resources, it has significant reserves of key resources that were vital to the start of the Industrial Revolution in the eighteenth century. Coal, iron ore and water were three highly significant resources that came together in the development of the first steam engine by James Watt in 1769. The invention of the steam engine changed the world for ever, providing industry with power and allowing the development of machinery for mass production. In the UK this led to rapid industrialisation, particularly in areas such as Nottingham where supplies of coal and water were plentiful.

Canals were built to transport coal, raw materials and finished products to and from the factories and mills. The canals were followed by the development of the railway network in the 1800s. The railways dramatically reduced journey times, allowing businesses and industry to flourish. The journey between London and Birmingham, for example, was reduced from almost 24 hours in 1821 (by stagecoach) to around four hours by train in 1845. The railways were also significant for the development of British colonies. Networks were built in India and eastern and southern Africa, easing the movement and export of raw materials to the UK where they were turned into manufactured goods.

Traditional industrial skills utilised local resources such as iron. This blacksmith is using his hammer to bend iron heated in a furnace.

FOSSIL FUELS

The UK's dependence on fossil fuels has changed little since the Industrial Revolution. In 2003 fossil fuels accounted for 89.8 per cent of the UK's energy needs. Coal, which met over 90 per cent of the UK's energy requirements in 1950, has since reduced in significance. By 2003 it accounted for only 17 per cent of UK energy. This decline was due to the exhaustion of the most accessible reserves and the increased costs of deep-mining, which made British coal more expensive than imported coal from countries such as the USA and Australia. In addition, the pollution from burning coal for heating and power was considered a primary cause of London's Great Smogs in 1952 and 1968, which led to the deaths of around 4,700 people. As a result of this the government introduced Clean Air Acts in 1956 and 1968 to reduce the use of coal in built-up areas. Since then most homes and businesses now use natural gas, a much cleaner fuel extracted from under the North Sea and Irish Sea.

GAS – PROS AND CONS

The UK now has around 90 gas fields supplying natural gas for domestic and industrial use and increasingly for electricity generation in gas-fired power stations. Natural gas does not emit sulphur dioxide (SO_2), which is one of the main gases responsible for producing acid rain and smog. Largely as a result of conversion to natural gas, emissions of SO_2 from UK cities have been cut by 60 per cent since 1960. However, natural gas is non-renewable – once used it cannot be replaced. Current UK reserves will probably be exhausted long before 2050. Natural gas also emits carbon dioxide (CO_2) when burnt – the main greenhouse gas responsible for global warming.

ENERGY RESOURCES

REDUCTION OF UK COAL PRODUCTION, 1970–2003

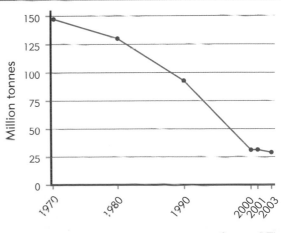

Source: DTI

CASE STUDY
UK OIL INDUSTRY

Ellesmere Port on the Mersey estuary is one of the UK's main oil refineries.

Oil was discovered in the UK under the North Sea in the early 1970s and first came into production in 1975. Its location, however, presented problems for extraction due to treacherous seas and the fact that the oil fields were a long distance from land. Platforms (oil rigs) were constructed to provide a stable surface for drilling into the seabed to extract the crude oil. The oil was then sent via special pipelines laid along the seabed to Sullom Voe, Europe's biggest oil refinery, on the Shetland Isles. Having overcome extraction difficulties the oil industry has grown rapidly and by 2003 the UK was the twelfth-biggest producer in the world, accounting for 2.9 per cent of the world total. Despite fears that North Sea oil (and gas) would run out shortly after the year 2000, recently discovered reserves are now being exploited. These reserves are expected to last until at least 2030. Extraction, however, is becoming more expensive as new supplies are discovered in increasingly remote locations. The UK will have to look to alternative sources of energy in the coming years if it is to continue to meet its own needs in the future.

REGIONAL RESOURCES

The UK has some regional natural resources and these have led to the development of localised and specialist industries in certain areas. For example, Cornwall in south-west England was historically a major producer of tin, whilst north Wales was the major source of slate used to make tiles for roofing. Many of these local industries have declined as resources became scarce or as new and cheaper alternatives became available. Slate tiles for example, were gradually replaced by manufactured clay tiles starting in the early 1900s. Today most of the slate mines have closed, although a few are now being turned into tourist attractions. One of the most famous regional industries in the UK was the pottery industry in Stoke-on-Trent, an area still known as 'the Potteries'.

The area around Stoke-on-Trent had the ideal combination of local clays and wood, and later coal fuel, needed to produce pottery. Specialist materials such as China clay from Cornwall were brought in using the region's canal network, which developed to meet the needs of the Potteries. Hundreds of small potteries sprang up in the area, identified by their bottle-shaped kilns, which dotted the landscape. The Clean Air Acts saw the end of the polluting bottle kilns, and many potteries closed as modern and highly mechanised technology was introduced. However, some of the most famous factories including Wedgwood and Royal Doulton continue to produce pottery, and their popularity with collectors around the world means they are also major tourist attractions.

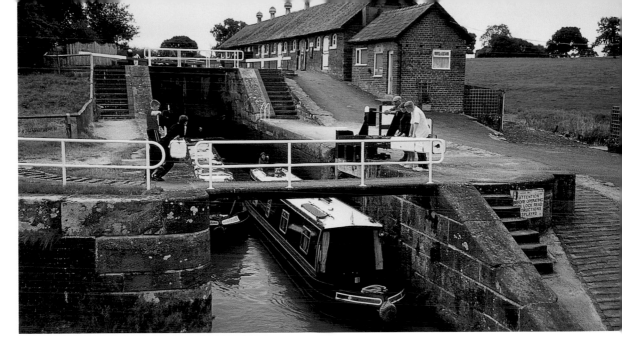

WATER RESOURCES

Historically, the UK's inland waterways played an important role in the Industrial Revolution. Today they are still significant, attracting more than 10 million visitors every year to enjoy boating, and walking or cycling along the old towpaths. Water is an important resource in other ways. Many large industries such as steel and paper manufacturing require large quantities of water during their production processes, and modern intensive farming uses irrigation to improve the growth and yield of

Canal holidays are increasingly popular with tourists such as these on the Trent and Mersey Canal, south of Manchester.

crops – especially vegetables. Water is also an important source of energy. Water wheels provided one of the earliest forms of energy and can still be seen in a few carefully preserved locations. Today the power of water is used to generate electricity in the form of hydroelectric power (HEP), as it passes through dams built across narrow river valleys. Scotland is the main producer of HEP in the UK, but the biggest single scheme is in north Wales at Dinorwig, near Llanberis.

The Wedgwood visitor centre near Stoke-on-Trent tells the story of the Potteries' development.

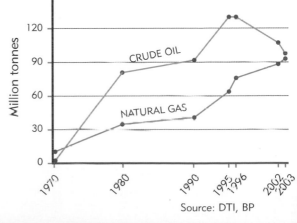

GROWTH IN UK OIL AND GAS PRODUCTION, 1970–2003

Source: DTI, BP

Silage making takes place in early summer. It is an important part of the dairy farmers' calendar.

OF LAND AND SEA

In addition to the resources extracted from the earth, the land and waters of the UK are important resources in themselves, supporting industries such as agriculture, forestry, fishing and tourism. In total UK agriculture meets around 60 per cent of food needs, despite employing only around 1 per cent of the labour force. Fertile soils enable intensive agricultural production of cereals such as wheat and barley, as well as fruit and vegetable crops such as carrots, potatoes, apples and berries. Other crops that are grown include flax, which is used to make linen, and rapeseed, which is pressed to obtain rapeseed oil. UK rapeseed cultivation has grown dramatically in recent years, increasing from just 274,000 tonnes in 1980 to 1,771,000 tonnes by 2003, making the UK the world's seventh-biggest producer.

CASE STUDY
UK FISHERIES

Fishermen sort through the daily catch at Whitby, Yorkshire.

The fisheries surrounding the UK are an important natural resource. However, in recent years many of the species caught have been in decline due to over-fishing by modern commercial fishing fleets. Cod is under particular pressure, with North Sea stocks down to around 10 per cent of their 1970 level. Cod stocks are likely to decline further still, with up to 85 per cent of the young fish being killed before they have matured and bred. In 1999 quotas (limits) on cod fishing were reduced by 90 per cent. Fishing fleets failed to catch even this amount, suggesting that stocks are much lower than predicted. The decline in fish stocks is affecting coastal communities around the UK, threatening family businesses that, in some cases, stretch back hundreds of years. In Scotland, hard-hit fishermen are facing an added threat to their livelihoods from the local seal population, which has grown from around 30,000 in 1978 to an estimated 120,000 in mid-2001. Fishermen estimate that grey seals consume 200,000 tonnes of fish from Scottish waters each year – more than the fishermen are allowed to catch. Fishermen are now arguing for a cull of seals to help protect fish stocks, but conservationists oppose the plan and say it will damage the tourist industry, which generates around £36 million per year from seal-watching tours.

Farmers haggle over the price of cattle at a market in Sussex.

Livestock rearing is important in the UK with sheep and cattle (for meat and milk) being the most significant, but pigs and poultry (mainly chickens) are also important. In recent years, however, the livestock industry has been troubled by falling prices and diseases such as BSE (mad cow disease) in cattle, and an outbreak of foot and mouth in 2001 (see pages 32–33).

Forestry in the UK is controlled by the Forestry Commission. The Forestry Commission was established in 1919 to manage British forests at a time when only 4 per cent of the UK was forest land. The conservation of remaining forests and replanting of trees for commercial use increased the forest cover in the UK to around 12 per cent by 2004.

RIGHT: Commercial forestry is carefully managed in the UK and forest cover is slowly increasing.

FOREST MANAGEMENT

Early forest plantations were almost entirely coniferous softwoods planted in uniform rows to make them easy to manage and harvest when mature (after about 50 years). Today plantations are less uniform and include a variety of deciduous trees and traditional species such as Scots pine. This change has been in recognition of the role that forests play in conserving environments and wildlife, and of their value to visitors. Many forests now contain walks or cycle paths for visitors to use.

POPULATION AND CHANGE

A CROWDED ISLAND

The UK is less than half the size of France, yet it has almost the same population. This makes the UK a very crowded island, with a population density in 2003 of 246 people per km², compared to 109 per km² in France and just 32 people per km² in the USA. However, people in the UK are not evenly distributed. The West Midlands of England, for example (the heart of the Industrial Revolution), has almost 3,000 people per km², compared to just 8 people per km² in the rugged Highland region of Scotland.

In urban areas population densities are much higher than in their rural surroundings. Oxfordshire and Norfolk are both rural counties with population densities below the national average and yet their principal towns of Oxford and Norwich have over 3,000 people per km². Among the most densely populated parts of the UK are the historic industrial cities such as Birmingham, Glasgow and Manchester. London is the most densely populated, with over 13,000 people per km² in districts such as Kensington and Chelsea.

POPULATION DENSITIES

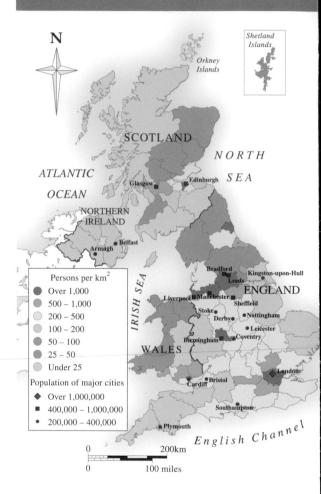

URBAN POPULATION (% OF TOTAL, 1950–2015)

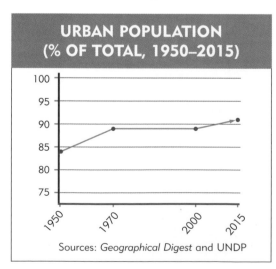

Sources: *Geographical Digest* and UNDP

POPULATION, 1950–2050

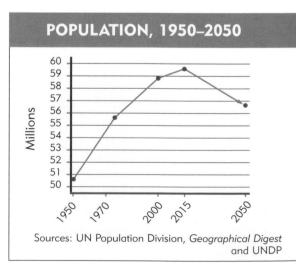

Sources: UN Population Division, *Geographical Digest* and UNDP

AN AGEING POPULATION

People in the UK are living longer than ever before because of dramatic improvements in healthcare and life expectancy during the last century. At the same time, young people are marrying later and having fewer children than before. This means that the total UK population is actually expected to decline by about 4 per cent between 2000 and 2050. However, the proportion of people over the age of 65 is expected to increase by 56 per cent over the same period, from about 16 per cent of the UK population in 2000 to around 19 per cent in 2015 and 25 per cent by 2050. This ageing of the UK population is starting to have significant impacts on the UK economy that are likely to become more severe in the coming decades. Healthcare systems are being stretched as they attempt to cope with more elderly patients needing care and employers in some areas are finding it increasingly difficult to find staff as fewer young people are entering the labour force. In the retail industry some firms are now employing people over the age of 65 on a part-time basis in order to fill this gap. Another dramatic impact on the UK economy is the increased demand for leisure and tourist activities from

People in the UK are living longer and enjoying greater leisure time in their retirement.

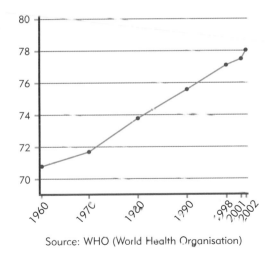

SOCIAL INDICATORS

UNDER-FIVE MORTALITY RATE (PER 1,000 LIVE BIRTHS)

Sources: UNICEF, UNDP and World Bank

LIFE EXPECTANCY AT BIRTH

Source: WHO (World Health Organisation)

older generations, which, with better health, increased mobility and higher incomes, are better able to enjoy their later life. The government calls this spending 'the grey pound' and also recognises the importance of keeping older generations content because of the growing power of 'the grey vote'.

If population growth continues to decline, the consequences for the UK would be dramatic. For example, if the working population were to be maintained at 1995 levels then the UK would require over 6 million additional migrant workers by 2050.

The UK today has many people of Asian origin. Birmingham is one city where they make up a large proportion of the population.

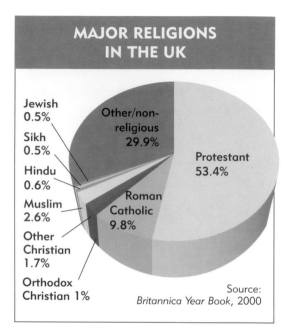

MAJOR RELIGIONS IN THE UK

Jewish 0.5%

Sikh 0.5%

Hindu 0.6%

Muslim 2.6%

Other Christian 1.7%

Orthodox Christian 1%

Other/non-religious 29.9%

Protestant 53.4%

Roman Catholic 9.8%

Source: Britannica Year Book, 2000

MIGRATION INTO THE UK

In the aftermath of the Second World War, the UK was desperately short of labour to help rebuild its tattered economy. Although the British themselves set about replenishing the population in a flurry of births that became known as 'the baby boom', there was still the immediate problem of labour shortages. This was met by government policies encouraging migrants to come to the UK from the former colonial territories of India and Pakistan, the Caribbean and British-controlled Africa. Hundreds of thousands of people arrived during the 1950s and 1960s, boosting the UK economy and settling, for the main part, in the UK's industrial cities.

By the early 1990s it was estimated that the UK had received about 4 million migrant residents accounting for around 7 per cent of the total population. As more migrants arrived in the UK they tended to settle close to those who arrived ahead of them, forming strong local communities that, in some cases, are almost entirely comprised of ethnic minority groups. Leicester, Bradford and Birmingham all have significant populations of Asian origin, whereas London has a particularly large number of people who were originally from the Caribbean and Africa. There has also been migration within the UK, with most movement being from Scotland, Wales and Northern Ireland into England.

A CULTURAL MELTING-POT

With the historical influence of the UK's colonial empire and the contemporary population mix since the 1950s, the UK has been described as a cultural melting-pot, where different beliefs, influences, tastes and ideas come together. This multi-cultural UK is strongest in the large cities, and centres such as Birmingham and Leicester are expected to be dominated by ethnic minority groups in the near future.

In some areas there have been conflicts caused by such ethnic differences. In the summer of 2001 several multi-ethnic communities in the north of England experienced violent street riots between white and Asian youths. Although such incidents are isolated and unusual they have raised concerns about the inequalities experienced by the UK's ethnic minorities. Ethnic minorities often experience higher levels of unemployment than their white neighbours and find work in lower-paid jobs. This in turn leads to lower standards of living, which may then further increase feelings of inequality.

The government is now looking at different ways to improve relations between such communities, with schools and young people playing a central role. Citizenship has been introduced into the national curriculum to encourage young people to accept and understand differences based not only on ethnic origin, but also as a result of religious beliefs or sexual orientation. It is hoped that such programmes will help everyone in the UK to understand the issues and enjoy the full benefits of a multi-cultural society.

RIGHT: Street carnivals, such as this one in Leeds, are a colourful element of the UK's multi-cultural society.
BELOW: Campaigners work to promote greater understanding between ethnic groups and reduce some of the tensions experienced in some communities.

SHARING CULTURES

The UK's multi-cultural society has influenced all areas of modern life: the most popular UK food is curry; African and Caribbean rhythms have had a strong impact on the UK music scene; Indian prints and fabrics have become popular in modern clothing design. This diversity has enriched life for most UK residents.

POPULAR CULTURE

Despite the wide variations within British culture there are certain elements that cut across such divides and have become known as 'popular culture'. Certain TV programmes, for example, appeal to a range of people from

Pavement cafés and restaurants are a sign of the UK's increasingly European culture.

very diverse backgrounds. Tastes in food, music and clothing are now shared by a broad cross-section of the British people. One aspect in particular has managed to cross social divides better than many others – sport. British people are among the world's most enthusiastic sports fans and follow their national and regional teams avidly. Football, rugby, cricket, athletics and tennis are among the most popular sports. Some of the UK's most successful sports people include Olympic winning athlete Kelly Holmes, footballers Wayne Rooney and David Beckham, and rugby player Jonny Wilkinson. Many of these sports stars recognise their ability to cross social and cultural barriers and have become

Chinese people have developed their own communities. This is a Chinese supermarket in China Town, Manchester.

involved in youth sports schemes that encourage people from all backgrounds to get involved.

Pop stars, too, are a big part of modern popular culture and again they manage to bridge social and cultural barriers. Many of the most popular recent acts include individuals from a broad range of ethnic backgrounds. In addition to its own multi-cultural influences, the UK's popular culture is also increasingly influenced by people and cultures from other countries. This is because modern communications and travel are allowing British people to experience previously remote people and places. The USA has perhaps had the biggest influence, particularly in the world of entertainment. Hollywood films and American TV shows such as *The Simpsons* are especially popular. However, influences from around the world can be seen, such as the recent trend for elements of Japanese culture – water gardens, bonsai trees and *feng shui*.

Bollywood films (the Indian equivalent of Hollywood) can be seen at Star City cinema, on the outskirts of Birmingham.

CASE STUDY
COOL BRITANNIA

With so many different cultures influencing the UK many people are now questioning exactly what it means to be British in the twenty-first century. Certain elements have remained very strong, however, such as the position of the Royal family and the use of the Union Jack flag as a symbol of the UK. In fact there was outrage when British Airways removed the Union Jack from its aircraft tails and a modern version of the flag was quickly reinstated. Other aspects of British culture are perhaps less obvious, but in the 1990s a new sense of Britishness began to emerge in a wave of new fashion, design, music and entertainment that became known as 'Cool Britannia'. This new image of the UK has embraced the diversity of the country, making it popular overseas as well as in the UK. Films such as *Four Weddings and a Funeral*, *East is East* and *Bridget Jones's Diary*, which deal with different aspects of British culture, have rejuvenated the British film industry. UK bands such as *Oasis* dominated the world music scene with many calling them 'The Beatles of the 1990s'. *Oasis* was just one of many UK bands that marked a revival in the British pop-music scene. Top models such as Naomi Campbell and Kate Moss, and designers such as Alexander McQueen have added to the image of Cool Britannia, which for many people in the UK has given them an identity they can be proud of.

Keeping up with the latest technology is essential to the economy. These people are checking circuit boards for computerised equipment.

A MODERN GLOBAL ECONOMY

Once the world's greatest economy, the UK was ranked only the fourth largest in 2003 and in terms of wealth per person the UK did not even make the top ten. However, the UK remains one of the most important economies in the world and London is still the world's most important financial centre. The UK economy has undergone drastic transformations since the 1950s and continues to do so as it modernises to compete in the global markets of the twenty-first century.

Modern businesses can locate almost anywhere in the world, conducting trade at the click of a button, and transferring money and information around the world in seconds. In such a fast-moving world the UK has to remain at the cutting edge of technology and enterprise if it is to maintain its position as a major world economy. The UK also faces the challenge of having to find alternatives to some of the traditional industries that have declined since the Second World War.

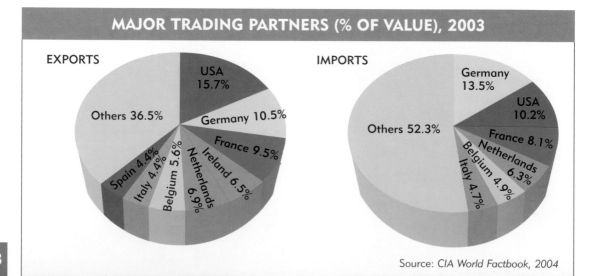

MAJOR TRADING PARTNERS (% OF VALUE), 2003

EXPORTS

- USA 15.7%
- Others 36.5%
- Germany 10.5%
- France 9.5%
- Ireland 6.5%
- Netherlands 6.9%
- Belgium 5.6%
- Italy 4.4%
- Spain 4.4%

IMPORTS

- Germany 13.5%
- USA 10.2%
- France 8.1%
- Netherlands 6.3%
- Belgium 4.9%
- Italy 4.7%
- Others 52.3%

Source: CIA World Factbook, 2004

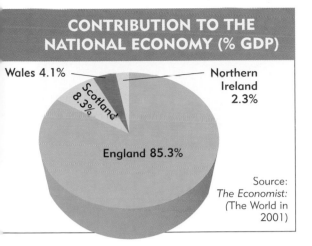

CONTRIBUTION TO THE NATIONAL ECONOMY (% GDP)

Wales 4.1%

Scotland 8.3%

Northern Ireland 2.3%

England 85.3%

Source: *The Economist:* (The World in 2001)

INDUSTRIES IN DECLINE

The heavy industries that formed the backbone of the UK economy since the Industrial Revolution have experienced rapid decline during the latter half of the twentieth century. Steel, shipbuilding, textiles and numerous other industries all but vanished from many parts of the UK, leaving land and buildings empty and derelict, and millions of skilled workers unemployed. In 1947, when the coal mines were nationalised (brought under government control), there were nearly 1,000 deep mines employing over 700,000 miners. By the time the government sold the industry to private companies (privatisation) in 1994 there were just 22 deep mines and 32 open-cast mines left, and employment had fallen to just 10,000 miners and support staff. Similar declines were commonplace across many traditional industries and where they still survive, such as the Potteries in

Stoke-on-Trent, production has been mechanised and the workforce cut to its bare minimum.

Although the UK's industrial decline has affected the whole economy, its biggest impact has been on those communities that developed around specific industries such as textiles in Manchester, steel in Sheffield or shipbuilding in Glasgow. The impact on these communities was made worse because many businesses were dependent on the main industry and its workers. This is known as a knock-on or multiplier effect. Just as many businesses were established to support the arrival of the industries and their workers (a positive multiplier) they have equally been forced to decline as unemployment increased and people had less money to spend in the local economy (a negative multiplier). The result of this has, in some places, been the collapse of entire communities, and parts of old industrial cities are now experiencing the highest poverty rates in the UK. In many instances the decline of industry and local communities has led to a depopulation of the area as people have moved away to look for work elsewhere. In Wales for example, the town of Blaenau Ffestiniog suffered a 95 per cent decrease in population following the decline and eventual closure of its slate quarry.

Slate spoil heaps dominate the old slate-mining community of Blaenau Ffestiniog, Wales.

Telecommunications, such as mobile phones, have played a major part in the growth of the UK's growing service economy in recent years.

A SERVICE ECONOMY

Today the UK economy is overwhelmingly dominated by the service sector, which accounted for 72.6 per cent of Gross Domestic Product (GDP – the value of goods and services produced in the UK) in 2003. The service sector includes any businesses or industries that offer services to people or other businesses. Banking and insurance are two of the biggest and oldest industries in this sector, but it also includes services such as leisure, tourism and the travel industry. These newer services have grown rapidly in recent years as a result of people having more leisure time, and new technologies making travel cheaper and easier.

THE CONSTRUCTION INDUSTRY

The construction industry reflects very strongly the overall state of the economy. When the economy is doing well both the government and private sector invest in new buildings or projects to extend or renovate existing property. However, if the economy starts to slow down then spending is often cut and the construction industry experiences a rapid decline as a result. Because of this, the construction industry makes use of a large number of casual employees who are employed as labourers according to the demand for workers at the time.

City redevelopment helps boost employment in the construction industry.

ECONOMIC STRUCTURE (% GDP)

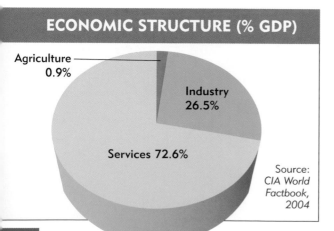

Agriculture
0.9%

Industry
26.5%

Services 72.6%

Source: CIA World Factbook, 2004

Other new technologies such as personal computers and mobile communications have also led to an increase in this sector, with growth in additional services such as training, support and the Internet. The speed of growth in these information technology (IT) services has been particularly rapid. Reports suggest that the demand for IT professionals in Europe outstripped supply by 600,000 in 2001 and that this figure could soon rise to around 2 million. The UK government is encouraging businesses to take a leading role in meeting such gaps by training people and developing what has become known as e-commerce (business that takes advantage of the Internet).

INDUSTRY AND MANUFACTURING

Industry accounts for most of the UK's remaining GDP, with construction, manufacturing and energy production being among the most important components. Within manufacturing the greatest contribution to the GDP was made by food products, printing and publishing, machinery, metal products and motor vehicle production. The UK is also a major producer of chemicals and is rapidly becoming a major centre for hi-tech electronics such as computer and telecommunications equipment. A large proportion of these new manufacturing industries are located in the south of England, while many of the old industries and areas of decline are in the north of the UK.

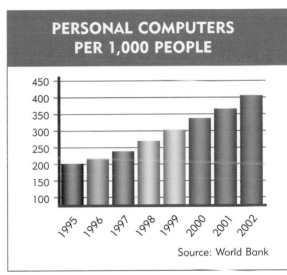

PERSONAL COMPUTERS PER 1,000 PEOPLE

Source: World Bank

The Mini, a classic British car, is now made by the German company BMW.

Increased competition in the motor industry has forced UK manufacturers into a period of restructuring over the last 20 years. Many smaller manufacturers have been taken over by bigger companies, such as Jaguar and Land Rover, now owned by Ford. The Mini is now made by BMW. In 2001 Rover was the only significant UK manufacturer remaining. The closure of plants and loss of jobs as a result of restructuring has been made up for by new investment from Japanese manufacturers deciding to locate their European plants in the UK. Nissan, Honda and Toyota have all built modern hi-tech plants in the UK to take advantage of the skilled labour force and government grants available. As a result of this investment from overseas, UK vehicle production has grown almost every year since 1986 and continues to employ an estimated 400,000 workers.

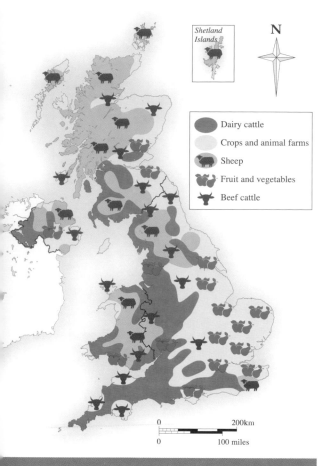

Shetland Islands

N

Dairy cattle
Crops and animal farms
Sheep
Fruit and vegetables
Beef cattle

0   200km
0   100 miles

AGRICULTURAL AREAS

Grazing cows are a typical UK countryside scene, but foot and mouth could have changed all that.

UK AGRICULTURE

Agriculture accounted for just 1.7 per cent of UK GDP in 1998 and employed only around 1 per cent of the labour force. In 2000, however, agriculture contributed to less than 1 per cent of the GDP for the first time in its history and the industry lost 20,000 workers – almost 6 per cent of the total agricultural workforce. Average farm incomes fell to a 25-year low of just £7,800, compared to their high of £25,000 in 1995. This crisis in British agriculture was partly caused by low agricultural prices and an increasingly global food industry in which the UK's traditionally small farms cannot compete. But it was also the result of two major livestock diseases – BSE (mad cow disease) and foot and mouth – which devastated not only the farms that were infected, but also confidence in UK farm produce. As the agricultural economy rebuilds itself, many feel it must use less intensive production methods and meet local food needs as part of a sustainable farming industry. This is starting to happen, with a 2,900 per cent increase in the area organically farmed during the period 1995–2003, and an increase in local farmers' markets and 'veggie-box' schemes, where farmers deliver produce direct to people's homes. Many people feel that the role of farmers as countryside managers should also be better emphasised.

The government is encouraging farmers to use their land in alternative ways such as for forestry or leisure facilities including golf courses, camping sites and rural attractions. Farmers are also being encouraged to manage the environment through policies such as 'set-aside', where land is left fallow, and meadows and natural animal and plant life are allowed to flourish. 'Buffer zones' are another such policy, where strips of land close to rivers and streams are left uncultivated to reduce pollution from chemicals and to provide a habitat for aquatic life. Rural campaign groups such as the UK Countryside Agency believe that farmers could use their land for even more diverse purposes in the future, such as for wind farms to generate renewable energy.

Straw bales are a familiar rural scene during harvest time (July–August).

CASE STUDY
FOOT AND MOUTH

Large parts of the UK were placed under strict disease control during the foot and mouth outbreak in 2001.

In February 2001 a case of foot and mouth disease was identified in England for the first time in 34 years. In the last outbreak (1967–1968) 440,000 animals were slaughtered, hundreds of jobs were lost and the economic cost was over £1.5 billion. By comparison, in 2001 a total of 3.6 million animals had been slaughtered by the end of July with an average of three new cases still being reported each day. The highly contagious nature of foot and mouth meant that the impact of the disease was felt throughout the UK. Footpaths and rural tourist attractions were closed and much of the British countryside became a no-go area. The outbreak worsened just as the tourist industry was preparing for its traditional Easter start, ending all hopes of a swift end to the crisis. By June 2001 it was estimated that foot and mouth disease had cost the UK economy between £10–20 billion. At least half these losses were in the leisure and tourism industries. Even traditional tourist centres such as Stratford-upon-Avon, the birth town of Shakespeare, have been affected despite not having a single case of foot and mouth disease. This town normally receives around 3.8 million visitors a year (second only to London) generating £135 million for the local economy and employing 17 per cent of the local labour force. In 2001, however, visitor numbers were estimated to be down by 30 per cent due to foot and mouth, causing hundreds of job losses and threatening many of the smaller business such as bed and breakfast cottages and restaurants.

TOURISM

The UK tourist industry accounted for 4.5 per cent of GDP in 2001, earning a total of £74 billion and employing around 2,100,000 people (7.4 per cent of all employment) in the UK. The majority of UK tourism is made up of domestic tourists and day-trippers, but the number of overseas visitors increased by 47 per cent between 1991 and 1999 and is expected to increase further still. The main tourist attractions in the UK include historic cities and houses, museums, industrial

Stratford-upon-Avon is a popular tourist destination because of its links with the famous playwright, William Shakespeare.

heritage centres, national parks, and countryside and theme parks. The residences of the Royal family are also a major attraction to overseas visitors, many of whom are keen to see anything with a royal connection. Alton Towers theme park in Staffordshire is the most popular fee-charging attraction, with 2.65 million visitors in 1999, closely followed by

CASE STUDY
OVERSEAS VISITORS

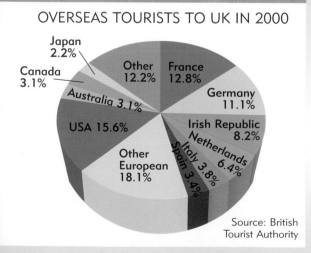

OVERSEAS TOURISTS TO UK IN 2000

Japan 2.2%
Canada 3.1%
Other 12.2%
France 12.8%
Germany 11.1%
Australia 3.1%
USA 15.6%
Irish Republic 8.2%
Netherlands 6.4%
Italy 3.8%
Spain 3.4%
Other European 18.1%

Source: British Tourist Authority

In 2000 25.2 million tourists visited the UK, making it the sixth most popular destination in the world, accounting for 4 per cent of the world's total number of tourists. Most visitors came from the USA and northern Europe, in addition to significant numbers from Australia, Canada and Japan. They stayed an average of 8.3 days and spent a total of £12.5 billion. Overseas tourism grew rapidly during the 1990s but in 2001 it suffered a set-back as foot and mouth disease meant large parts of the countryside became difficult to move about in. In addition, a slow-down in the global economy led to a reduction in overseas bookings from countries such as the USA, which accounted for almost 16 per cent of visitors in 2000.

Madame Tussaud's waxworks museum and the Tower of London. Many tourist attractions are free, however, such as national parks or historic towns. This type of tourism is on the increase as places throughout the UK try to cash in on the growing number of visitors. Stratford-upon-Avon has long used its Shakespeare connection to encourage tourism, whilst Ironbridge, to the north-west of Birmingham, markets itself as the birthplace of the Industrial Revolution. Even small villages can benefit from their historical past: the Derbyshire village of Eyam advertises itself as the site of a plague outbreak in 1665 that claimed over 70 per cent of the village's population. There is also a very modern type of tourism that uses the UK's revived reputation as 'Cool Britannia'. This appeals to a large number of fashion-conscious and mainly young tourists who have made cities such as Brighton and Manchester popular as much for their 'cool' culture and image as anything else. This can be seen in the number of designer shops, street cafés and night-clubs that have sprung up in these cities.

DOMESTIC TOURISM

In 2001 there were around 161 million domestic tourists in the UK, making up 87.5 per cent of the total. They spent an amazing £59 billion, most of which paid for stays of only one or two nights. City breaks account for nearly 65 per cent of all visits. A further £33.4 billion was spent on day-trips taken in the UK in 2001; by 2004, this figure had risen to £34.2 billion. These day-trips do not officially count as tourist visits because they do not involve a stay away for a night, but they are important because they account

Dovedale, with its stepping stones, is one of the most popular parts of the Peak District.

for over half of all earnings from tourism. National parks (see page 55) such as the Lake District or the Brecon Beacons in South Wales are popular destinations for day-trippers. The Peak District is one of the most popular attractions because of its location within easy reach of major cities such as Manchester, Sheffield and Nottingham. With an estimated 30 million day visitors each year the Peak District is beaten only by Mount Fuji in Japan as the most visited national park in the world.

Donkey rides on Blackpool beach are a popular treat for young visitors to the area.

THE 'OUT-OF-TOWN' ECONOMY

While the UK economy used to rely heavily on the physical location of resources, today it depends more on issues such as transport links and ease of customer access. This has given rise to an 'out-of-town' economy, where an increasing number of businesses, industries and services are choosing to locate away from town centres on large open areas of land, often close to major road networks. Business, science, industrial, retail and leisure parks are now a common sight around much of the UK, and in some places they can all be found within a single location. Many of the businesses that locate at these parks are large companies with many outlets or factories around the country or even internationally. Small and local businesses are unable to compete and, as their customers begin to use out-of-town facilities, many have been forced to close down. Even large companies have closed their town centre locations in favour of out-of-town sites, leaving shops, offices and factories abandoned and boarded up in many town centres.

The growing trend of large companies to move away from the town centres has taken its toll on some local economies. Since the late 1990s some town centres have undergone extensive renovations in an attempt to revitalise the local economy. Transport and parking facilities have been improved, purpose-built shopping malls developed and offices modernised or rebuilt to take advantage of the latest technology. Even within these redevelopments, however, it is often large companies that benefit while local independent businesses are increasingly vulnerable.

RISING EMPLOYMENT LEVELS

Despite changes and unemployment black-spots, the overall trend in the UK has been one of increasing employment. In 2001 unemployment fell to below 5 per cent. The number of people claiming unemployment benefit fell below 1 million for the first time since 1975, having peaked at over 3 million in 1986. This turn-around in employment levels is considered by many to be a sign that the UK has overcome the economic declines of the past and is now emerging as a modern economy better able to compete in the new global marketplace.

EMPLOYMENT

Changes in the economy are reflected in UK employment figures. Employment in heavy industry and manufacturing has declined significantly, while the proportion of people working in the service sector grew to 73 per cent by 2001. Agriculture employs only around 1 per cent of the working population – even the UK's energy sector has more employees.

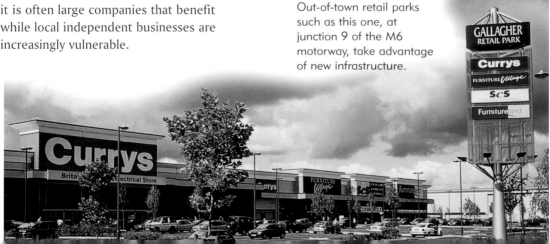

Out-of-town retail parks such as this one, at junction 9 of the M6 motorway, take advantage of new infrastructure.

Shopping malls, with many different shops under the same roof are replacing traditional high street shops.

TELECOMMUNICATIONS DATA
(PER 1,000 PEOPLE)

Mainline Phones	591
Mobile Phones	841
Internet Users	423

Source: World Bank

The location of employment has also changed, with the south of England having the highest employment levels, while many old industrial areas and inner cities have high unemployment. In parts of Wales nearly half of the people of working age are unemployed, while in Liverpool 65 per cent of 16–24 year olds are unemployed. The workforce is also changing. The proportion of women in employment has grown by just over 10 per cent since 1965, although 44 per cent of these jobs are part-time compared to just 9 per cent for men. More people are also choosing to work for themselves. The UK had an estimated 3.3 million people in self-employment in 2003 accounting for over 12 per cent of all employment. Technology such as faxes, e-mail and the Internet also led to an estimated 2 million people working from home by mid-

A job centre in Blaenau, Wales. This area had the highest unemployment levels in the UK in 2001.

2001. This trend is likely to continue as even large businesses are beginning to allow employees to use such technology to work from home while staying in contact with the office and their colleagues. These new work patterns also benefit the environment as they involve less travel and a more efficient use of space.

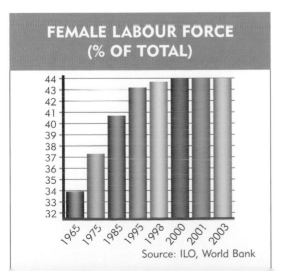

FEMALE LABOUR FORCE (% OF TOTAL)

Source: ILO, World Bank

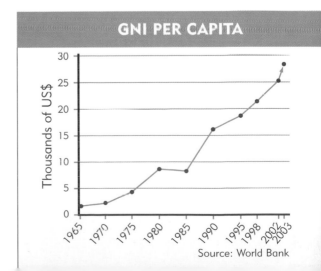

GNI PER CAPITA

Source: World Bank

TRANSPORT AND INFRASTRUCTURE

Traffic jams on the M25 motorway are a common sight, especially in the evening rush hour.

It is perhaps not surprising that in a country with a strong motoring history the car is something of a star in the UK, but the extent to which the car dominates transport is a cause for concern. Cars (and other motor vehicles) are among the biggest contributors to the UK's greenhouse gas emissions and road accidents are the leading cause of death in young people under 15 years old. Despite such problems, British people are using cars more than ever before and the number of cars on the road is increasing.

In 2003 there were an estimated 31.2 million vehicles on the UK's roads, 80 per cent of which were private cars. This represented a 70 per cent increase in the number of vehicles since 1980. As patterns of living and working continue to change, car use is expected to increase by as much as 50 per cent by 2025. With so many vehicles the UK's road network has expanded dramatically over the years and now covers a total distance of 371,913km – only 12,000km short of the distance between the Earth and the Moon. However, traffic congestion remains a major problem in many parts of the UK and is estimated to cost the economy around £15 billion each year in lost time and production. Congestion has been made worse by people using cars for even the shortest of trips.

CAR DEPENDENCY

Nearly half of all car journeys in the UK are less than 3km – a distance that could easily be covered by using public transport, cycling or walking. The car is such a part of British life that there are over 46 cars for every 100 people. This is less than in France or Germany, but the growth in UK car ownership has been especially high at 67 per cent between 1980 and 2001, compared to 63 per cent in Germany and just 37 per cent in France.

Train use is increasing again, but delays and technical problems are still common on many routes.

UK RAILWAYS

The railway network is the most popular alternative to the car for long-distance travel, and connects most major towns and cities in the UK. Developed initially for trade and industry, the railway became a popular mode of public transport from the 1830s and was significant in the early development of tourism in the UK. Trains such as the 'Southern Belle', which ran between London and Brighton until 1933 increased the popularity of tourism by train. The route is still one of the most popular today. Just as the railways replaced the canal network as the main form of transporting cargo, roads have since replaced the railways for all but the bulkiest of goods and many railway lines have closed as a result. Some are maintained as tourist attractions, with restored steam engines providing experiences of a time gone by. Others have been converted into cycle tracks, such as in the Manifold Valley in Derbyshire.

The UK's main railway network was privatised in 1994 and was operated by a number of companies in different parts of the country. There were numerous problems as these operators and the owner of the tracks and signals (Railtrack) attempted to modernise the network to encourage greater use of trains. The biggest problems were caused by mechanical faults and delays to services, but a series of major accidents also raised concern about the safety of the railways. In October 2001 Railtrack collapsed and the railway network returned to government control.

MAIN TRANSPORT NETWORKS

INTEGRATED TRANSPORT SYSTEMS

The key challenge for modern transport policy is to encourage what the government calls 'integrated transport systems'. These are transport systems that reduce problems of congestion and pollution associated with greater road use, but at the same time allow people and goods to move around more efficiently and flexibly. The key to such systems is getting different modes of transport to work together. This already occurs to some extent in terms of moving freight. Packing freight into standardised containers (containerisation) means that the same container can be moved more easily from trains to lorries and ships. Transport 'hubs' provide meeting places for the different forms of transport to transfer the containers. These transport hubs are located in key centres such as ports and industrial cities.

Providing such a system for passenger transport is less straightforward. People are widely distributed and their travel needs are extremely varied, but regular services providing connections between different

Manchester's Metrolink is part of one of the most successful integrated transport systems in the UK so far.

forms of transport have been successful in many cities. In Belfast for example, the Europa Bus Centre and Great Victoria Street Railway Station provide an efficient connection between the bus and rail systems. One of the most successful integrated transport systems is the Greater Manchester Metrolink, which provides regular city centre trams that connect with local and regional bus services. The Metrolink carries 18.8 million passengers a year and prevents around 2 million car journeys travelling into the city centre each year. Similar systems exist or are being constructed in Birmingham, Sheffield, Nottingham and several other cities.

RURAL TRANSPORT

Providing integrated transport for people living in rural areas is more problematic. Low population densities in these areas mean that providing rural services is less profitable for transport companies. As a result, many rural bus services have been reduced to only a few times a week whilst others have been lost altogether. Dial-a-bus schemes (where people can telephone in advance to order a bus service) have been introduced in some areas in an attempt to bring services and demand together, but in rural areas most people tend to use their car for transport. One solution would be to make cars less environmentally harmful. Cleaner fuels such as liquid petroleum gas (LPG) are already on the market, as are specially designed cars that combine petrol and electric engines. The main hope for the future, however, is in hydrogen-powered cars using special fuel cells that release only water vapour but provide the same power as current petrol engines. Buses using this system are already in use in Canada and it is hoped that the first cars using hydrogen fuel cells will be available in the UK in 2005.

Buses are the main form of transport for the 30 per cent of British people who do not have a car.

CASE STUDY
NATIONAL CYCLE NETWORK

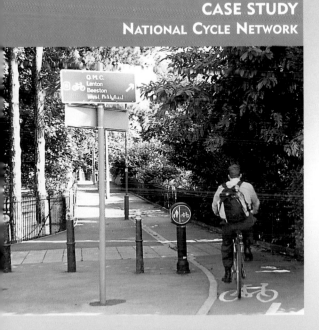

The National Cycle Network is intended to contribute to a new era of sustainable travel.

Cycle use in the UK declined by 36 per cent between 1986 and 1998, despite the fact that there are more bicycles in the UK than cars. Many people are concerned about riding bicycles along increasingly polluted and congested roads. The National Cycle Network hopes to reverse this trend by establishing a nationwide network of cycle paths and cycle-friendly roads to make cycling safer. The first 9,600km of the network were opened in the summer of 2000 and a further 6,400km are planned for completion by 2005. The network is intended to benefit commuters, shoppers, children going to school and tourists who want to enjoy an alternative and healthy way of visiting different parts of the UK. Sign-posted routes, and links with railway stations and major population centres will put about 30 million people within easy reach of the network when it is complete.

Regular exercise is a good way of keeping fit and healthy.

UNHEALTHY TRENDS

Although people in the UK are living longer than ever before, they are not necessarily healthier. In fact the health of the nation shows some worrying trends, such as growing rates of obesity and falling levels of exercise. Such trends are linked to changing lifestyles. Watching television, for example, is the UK's favourite leisure activity, especially among younger generations. The average amount of time spent watching television doubled between 1965 and 2003 to 26 hours a week.

People are consuming more high fat and high sugar foods such as burgers, pizzas, crisps and sweets than in previous decades. These foods are high in calories and have contributed to an estimated 51 per cent of adults in the UK being overweight. The proportion of people who are severely overweight (obese) has doubled since 1990. Such problems are not limited to adults. Obesity amongst young people and even toddlers in the UK has increased dramatically in recent years. Recent reports suggest that nearly 25 per cent of children under four years old are overweight and almost 10 per cent are obese. This recently named 'Teletubby generation' could have a serious impact on future UK healthcare spending.

DANGERS OF A POOR DIET

The 'Teletubby generation' could place a serious strain on the health service in the future, adding to the estimated £2.6 billion a year that obesity currently costs the UK economy and health system. There are already signs that diabetes is associated with obesity. Poor diet is increasing amongst teenagers, and other diet-related illnesses such as heart disease and strokes are among the UK's biggest causes of death.

A HEALTH CRISIS

When the National Health Service (NHS) was set up in 1948 it was considered the envy of the world, providing free medical care to everyone in the UK. In the 1990s, however, the NHS came under increasing criticism as rural and small-town hospitals were closed, and patients had to wait longer to be treated. The growing elderly population and the decline in the health of the population as a whole put the NHS under extreme pressure. In late 2003 there were just over 950,000 people waiting for treatment.

The ageing population is a particular strain, as shown by the increase in demand for replacement joints such as hips and knees to improve life for elderly people whose natural joints have worn out. Some patients are forced to wait for over a year just to get on to a waiting list for an operation, a fact that annoys many elderly patients in particular, having paid into the NHS (through taxes) for their whole working lives.

The government is investing more money in hospitals and in the training of new health staff, but an increasing number of people are turning to private medical care instead. Such services are not an option for the poorest and most vulnerable in society, however, and many people have little choice but to wait for treatment on the NHS.

Some experts suggest that not eating a balanced diet that includes fresh fruit and vegetables and other important foods can contribute to poor general health.

The time that people wait for care varies dramatically across the UK. In Cardiff, Wales, 45 per cent of people have to wait over six months for an operation, compared to just 0.5 per cent of those living in Dorset, southern England. The most unhealthy regions of the UK are those areas where poverty is also greatest. This means that those areas with the greatest need for health services are the least able to afford them. Glasgow is one of the worst-affected cities. People living in the poorest areas of Glasgow are three-and-a-half times more likely to die before the age of 65 than those living in Cambridgeshire or Surrey, which are wealthy counties.

The government is investing in healthcare to rebuild confidence in the NHS.

POVERTY AND PLENTY

People living in poverty in the UK normally have lower education standards and poorer housing conditions than people living in wealthier communities. Poverty is also closely linked to unemployment and so tends to be highest in former industrial and manufacturing centres where employment has been declining. The division between richer and poorer areas in the UK is sometimes known as the north-south divide, the north being generally poorer than the south. In the north-west of England for example, the average weekly income per person in 1998 was £145, compared with £207 in south-eastern England. Wales and Scotland were in between these levels at £151 and £158 per week respectively, whilst Northern Ireland had the lowest weekly income at just £126 per person. Such figures are only indicators, however, and do not reveal the differing levels of wealth within these regions. Elderly people are among the poorest members of communities throughout the UK. Nearly a quarter of pensioners were living in poverty in 2003. The poorest group are single parent families, with around 53 per cent living in poverty in 2002.

BELOW: In major cities local authorities often house people in tower blocks, but these sometimes lead to greater exclusion from the wider community.

TEENAGE PREGNANCY

The UK has seen a growth in the number of teenage pregnancies and currently has the highest rate in Europe. Every year about 90,000 teenagers in England become pregnant (resulting in 56,000 births), including nearly 8,000 girls under 16 and 2,200 girls aged 14 or younger. This is a worrying trend because many of these girls may not complete their education and learn the skills needed to find employment.

Teenage pregnancy is one of the causes behind the growth in single parents in the UK.

EDUCATION, EDUCATION, EDUCATION

Better education is considered by many to be the main way to reduce poverty and improve the state of society in the UK. Unemployed people, for example, are twice as likely to have low literacy skills as those in paid employment, suggesting that better education would help them find employment and therefore reduce their poverty. Schooling is compulsory in the UK until the age of 16, but the quality of education received varies dramatically. In some areas school absenteeism is a major problem. The worst-performing schools tend to be located in the poorest areas, meaning that children in these areas are less likely to attain enough qualifications for a well-paid job. The challenge is to break this poverty cycle and provide young people in disadvantaged areas with opportunities to improve their education and skills. The UK government has made this its major task for the future. Prime Minister Tony Blair's famous slogan of 'education, education, education' was used repeatedly in the build-up to his party's election victory in June 2001. Schools are being equipped with computers to teach new skills for the twenty-first century and schools in disadvantaged areas are being given specialist teachers to help motivate individual pupils and improve their performance.

One of the government's main aims is to improve the quality of education in the UK.

INCOME INEQUALITY

The gap between the poorest and the richest people in the UK has widened since the 1980s. This led to higher income inequality in the UK in the late 1990s than at any time since the fifteenth century. In 1979 the richest 10 per cent (decile) of the population enjoyed 20 per cent of the UK's total income whilst the poorest decile shared just 4.1 per cent. By 1999 the share in total income had risen to 28 per cent for the richest decile, but fallen to just 2 per cent for the poorest. This growing inequality is even more striking if real incomes are considered. Weekly incomes for the poorest decile fell by 12 per cent between 1979 and 1996 whilst those of the wealthiest decile increased by 68 per cent, providing evidence that 'the rich get richer whilst the poor get poorer'.

Grafitti covers a wall in Brighton, East Sussex.

THE BIG ISSUE

In 1991 a magazine called *The Big Issue* was launched as a self-help programme for homeless people to earn money. *The Big Issue* now sells over 250,000 copies and is read by a million people each week. Apart from the financial rewards, the Big Issue Foundation assists people in rebuilding their lives with the help of training or counselling to allow them to play an active role in society again.

The Big Issue has proven a great success in helping the most vulnerable homeless people.

SOCIAL EXCLUSION

Poor health, low education standards, poverty, family break-ups and unemployment are often found in the same location. They can combine to cause so many social problems that communities and individuals become excluded from wider society because of their circumstances. Many people living in deprived inner cities such as Glasgow and Liverpool face 'social exclusion'. Young people find it particularly difficult to cope with such situations. In the worst cases, exclusion can lead to problems of drug and alcohol abuse or leave people homeless and living rough on the streets.

In 2002–03 an estimated 129,000 households were classified as homeless in the UK, mainly due to family break-downs or failure to keep up rent payments. Most of these people are taken into the care of local authorities, but this is not always the case, and some end up living rough and may be seen begging for money on the streets of major cities.

CRIME AND PREVENTION

Social exclusion, poverty and unemployment have often been blamed for an increase in crime in the UK in recent decades. Theft, burglaries and car crime have all increased since the 1970s, as have attacks on people related to robberies. Some of the worst-affected areas are also those facing the greatest levels of poverty and unemployment.

An increase in police officers and the introduction of closed circuit television (CCTV) cameras is starting to reduce crime and in 2001 the overall crime rate was 2.5 per cent lower than in 2000. Car theft and burglaries fell furthest by 7.2 and 7.8 per cent respectively, but robbery increased by 12.9 per cent, especially that of mobile phones, which accounted for almost 40 per cent of robberies in some urban areas. Despite some improvements, there were still a total of 5.2 million crimes reported in the UK between 2000 and 2001, of which only 24 per cent were solved by the police.

CASE STUDY
BIG BROTHER

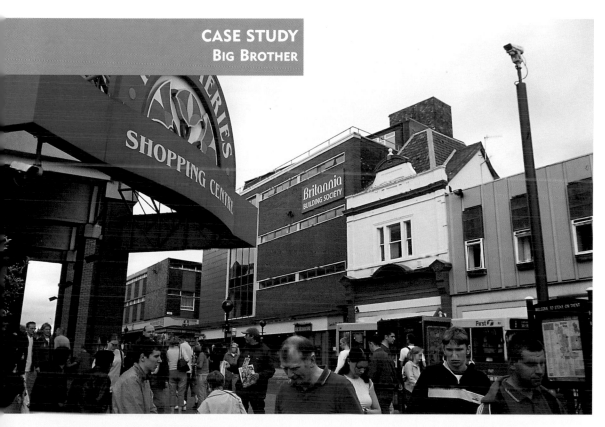

CCTV cameras in Stoke-on-Trent, West Midlands, capture the movements of shoppers on a busy Saturday afternoon.

A television series called *Big Brother* was one of the most popular shows between 2000 and 2004. The series was based on a house in which the occupants' daily life was followed by numerous video cameras around the clock and then broadcast on the Internet and nightly TV shows. The idea of cameras following people constantly is becoming a reality in the UK. The UK has the largest network of CCTV cameras in the world. The cameras are concentrated in cities (150,000 in London alone), but most urban areas and small towns now have some form of CCTV. The cameras are installed to make the streets safer and reduce levels of theft and vandalism. Each day, an average city-dweller is filmed at least eight (and up to 300) times.

This has led some people to see CCTV systems as an intrusion on privacy. The latest systems are even capable of matching people's faces against police records, using sophisticated computers to identify known criminals. The introduction of such a system in the London borough of Newham saw crime fall by 34 per cent in six months, proving to many that CCTV is extremely valuable. With more cameras being installed every year, the idea of a 'Big Brother' watching people's every move may soon become very real.

Beautiful environments such as the Yorkshire Dales are protected so that everyone can enjoy them.

GROWING CONCERN

Concern for the environment in the UK is reaching new heights. More and more people are becoming members of environmental groups such as Greenpeace or Friends of the Earth. This concern is also evident on the streets, where there are more environmentally friendly products for sale, higher rates of recycling and increasing demand for organic food.

Such attitudes are mainly due to people being better informed about the condition of the environment, but also because people have greater leisure time to enjoy and care for their surroundings. Some people, however, have suggested that concern for the environment is a luxury for the better-off in society and that poorer communities and individuals (who often suffer the worst environments) do not have time to share in such luxuries.

The UK government is taking environmental issues more seriously than ever before and implementing various new policies that force or encourage people to help protect the environment. A new vehicle tax system, for example, charges higher taxes to those with bigger, more polluting vehicles, whilst drivers who convert to using cleaner technologies such as liquid petroleum gas (LPG) instead of petrol are supported by government grants. Both of these policies are part of the government's commitment to reduce emissions of carbon dioxide (CO_2) – one of the main greenhouse gases responsible for global warming.

Electric buses, such as this one covering a city centre route in Birkenhead, near Liverpool, are one way to reduce dependence on carbon.

REDUCING GREENHOUSE GASES

Much of the UK economy relies on technologies that produce large quantities of CO_2. Almost 90 per cent of the UK's energy comes from fossil fuels, which emit vast quantities of CO_2 when they are burnt. The UK's dependence on motor vehicles also adds to this burden. In 2001 motor vehicle emissions were the fastest-growing contributor to greenhouse gases. With car use predicted to increase by 17 per cent by 2010 the trend is set to continue. Similar patterns can also be seen in most industrial nations of the world and as the economies of developing nations grow, they, too, are emitting an increasing amount of CO_2. This resulted in all of the world's leaders coming together in Kyoto in Japan in 1997 to agree action that would reduce pressure on the global environment in the coming years. The UK agreed to reduce its greenhouse gas emissions to 12.5 per cent below their 1990 levels by 2010, focusing on renewable energy as the best way of achieving this target.

RENEWABLE ENERGY

In 2003 renewable energy accounted for almost 3 per cent of the UK's electricity generation, but this was twice as much as in 1993 and the renewable energy sector grew by 8 per cent in 2000 alone. Renewable energy is set to grow very rapidly in the next decade or so, with the government setting targets for it to meet 10 per cent of all needs by 2010. At present the vast majority of renewable energy (87 per cent) comes from biofuels such as landfill gas, refuse combustion and industrial wood burning. Hydroelectricity (HEP) provides 8.6 per cent whilst wind power, the only other major source, provided just 3.4 per cent of renewable energy in 2003.

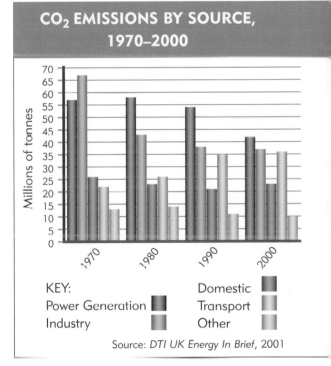

CO₂ EMISSIONS BY SOURCE, 1970–2000

Millions of tonnes

KEY:
Power Generation
Industry
Domestic
Transport
Other

Source: *DTI UK Energy In Brief*, 2001

Solar panels are used to power some parking meters, such as this one in Nottingham.

CASE STUDY
WIND FARMS

In 2004 the UK had around 84 wind farms. These wind farms generated about 655 megawatts (MW) of power in total, enough for 441,000 homes. Studies have shown that the UK has the world's highest potential wind power resource – Scotland alone has more than the whole of Europe. Despite this seemingly obvious source of renewable and emission-free energy, wind power has yet to really take off in the UK. One of the problems is that while people may agree with the idea of wind power, they object to turbines being located near their homes – an attitude that has become known as the 'Not In My Back Yard' (NIMBY) syndrome. Complaints about noise are the most common, but turbines are also blamed for spoiling scenic views, affecting radio and television signals, and posing a threat to birds. Some communities have learnt to live with wind turbines, however, such as the people of Swaffham in Norfolk. Their 98m-high wind turbine has become a local landmark. The turbine attracts thousands of tourists who come to learn about wind power and other sustainable technologies.

One solution to complaints about wind turbines is to locate them offshore – a technique already used in Denmark. In 2004 the UK had 32 offshore wind turbines, with

Tourists pay to climb the Ecotricity wind turbine in Swaffham, Norfolk, the only one in the UK with a viewing platform.

hundreds more planned for construction. When finished, these turbines will provide a total of 7,000 MW of power. This could make offshore wind farms a major source of energy for the UK in the coming years.

WASTE AND RECYCLING

In 2001–2002, 77 per cent of the UK's municipal waste was disposed of in landfill sites and a further 9 per cent was incinerated. This means that only 14 per cent of the UK's municipal waste was recycled or composted, compared with over 32 per cent in Denmark and Sweden, and almost 50 per cent in the Netherlands. Such low levels of recycling may have a major impact on the UK's environment.

Landfill sites can contain hazardous materials that take hundreds or even thousands of years to break down. As these materials break down, they release chemicals that mix with water passing through the landfill to form leachate. Leachate can pass into local water supplies, contaminating the environment and making its way into drinking-water supplies. Landfills also generate methane gas as waste decomposes, or breaks down.

WIND ENERGY SITES IN THE UK

N

Shetland Islands

Orkney Islands

SCOTLAND

NORTH SEA

Y Wind farms

NORTHERN IRELAND

IRISH SEA

ENGLAND

WALES

0   200km

0   100 miles

English Channel

Methane is a major greenhouse gas and is also highly explosive if not carefully managed. Modern landfills are lined to prevent leachate escaping and have special vents to release methane, but the real solution is to landfill less waste, especially since the UK is running out of landfill space. In recent years incineration has become a more favoured option to landfill because burning waste reduces its bulk by about 90 per cent. However, concern about the safety of emissions from incinerators has led to a backlash from environmentalists and concerned residents. The concern surrounds wastes containing toxic organic micro pollutants (TOMPs) which, unless burnt at over 1,200°C, release toxins into the environment. Some of these toxins have been linked to cancer and birth defects in humans, and deformities and premature deaths in wildlife (especially birds). The latest incinerators are highly efficient and their designers claim to have eradicated these emissions. However, fears concerning the health effects of incinerators mean they will probably meet continued resistance from UK residents.

Most of the UK's municipal waste is disposed of in landfill sites like this one at Rainham, Essex.

The Centre for Alternative Technology in Machynlleth, Wales was one of the first to start educating people about better environmental management.

THE THREE RS

The debate over whether to landfill or incinerate waste in the UK has detracted from the real issue concerning waste, the so-called 'three Rs' – Reduce, Re-use and Recycle. There is a need for the UK to reduce the amount of waste it produces in the first place, to re-use materials and objects wherever possible, and then, if they have no further use, to recycle them instead of disposing of them. Items such as envelopes, glass jars and paper can easily be re-used around the household. Some companies offer specialist re-use facilities such as 'Ink Again', which re-uses old ink cartridges from printers, refilling them to provide cheaper replacements than original parts. Recycling is already practised by most households in the UK, although it is often limited to glass bottles and newspaper, which are collected from the kerbside or taken to special recycling collection points. Other waste products such as cardboard, plastics, metals and old clothing can be recycled into

new products or used as the raw material for other objects. Plastic soda bottles marked with the letters PET, for example, are the raw material used to make fleece jackets, whilst a single plastic vending machine cup can be made into a pencil by a UK company called Remarkable Pencils. Composting is another form of recycling that could be greatly improved in the UK. About 40 per cent of the average household's waste is biodegradable, meaning it can be broken down by natural organisms. If composted instead of being thrown away, biodegradable waste provides a valuable fertiliser for the garden and reduces the UK's waste burden.

Perhaps the most difficult of the three Rs to achieve is reducing the level of waste produced in the first instance. The UK is a consumer nation where people want the latest fashions, newest designs and most up-to-date technology, even if they have existing goods that are still useable. In some cases, however, replacing goods can be beneficial for the environment. A modern washing machine, for example, uses about a third of the electricity and half as much water as a machine made in the 1970s.

This energy-efficient office building in Wales is built from recyclable materials and uses renewable solar power to generate electricity.

CASE STUDY
GLASS RECYCLING

Glass is a particularly good material for recycling as it can be used to make up to 90 per cent of new glass, saving both energy and resources. Compared to manufacturing glass with raw materials, recycling glass reduces air pollution by 20 per cent, mining wastes by 80 per cent and water consumption by 50 per cent. Over 6 billion glass containers are used in the UK each year, but only 22 per cent of them are currently recycled, compared to the European average of 50 per cent. With over 22,000 bottle banks around the UK there is little excuse for people not to recycle glass.

There are, however, some problems concerning glass recycling. Around 60 per cent of the glass recycled in the UK is coloured, whereas 70 per cent of manufactured glass is clear, so there is a mismatch between supply and demand. One solution already in use in the USA is to colour bottles using a thin film that disappears when the glass is melted down, instead of colouring the glass itself. This 'ColorCoat' technology also removes the need to sort glass into different colours at bottle banks.

The UK has very poor rates of recycling compared with its European neighbours.

Park-and-ride schemes have been introduced by numerous authorities in the UK to reduce urban traffic pollution.

A SUSTAINABLE FUTURE?

Sustainable development is defined as meeting the needs of the present population without harming the ability of future generations to meet their needs. The UK government is committed to meeting these objectives and it attempts to ensure that its policies work towards such goals. The government introduced a landfill tax to deter people from dumping waste and to encourage them to think about alternative ways to manage it. Education and awareness about sustainable development are also important. The government has set up a national advertising campaign and website called 'Doing Your Bit' as well as introducing sustainable development into the school curriculum. Local authorities are also working towards a more sustainable future by introducing policies as part of Local Agenda 21, a guideline for working towards internationally agreed goals to achieve sustainable development. Park-and-ride schemes, bus and cycle lanes, recycling collections, sustainable housing programmes, and the protection and regeneration of environments are all examples of policies introduced to meet Local Agenda 21.

PROTECTED AREAS

Whilst local authorities can protect and regenerate local environments, the UK has certain environments that are considered of national or even international importance. These areas are protected as national parks or as specially designated Areas of Outstanding Natural Beauty (AONB) or Sites of Special Scientific Interest (SSSI). In Scotland protected areas are referred to as National Scenic Areas.

In 1951 the Peak District was the first national park to be established in the UK: it covers an area of 1,438km^2 between the cities of Manchester and Sheffield. Since then a further twelve national parks have been established, and two more national parks were proposed for England in 2001.

SSSIs can be relatively small areas, such as ponds or meadows that are habitats for endangered species or have special geographical interest. SSSIs can be located within national parks as they have special regulations regarding their protection. AONB are areas considered worthy of protection for their natural scenery, but they do not normally have the same level of protection as national parks. The South Downs

in Sussex is listed as an AONB but will soon become one of the UK's new national parks.

Whilst protected areas are intended to be enjoyed by tourists, the enormous increase in tourism is placing increasing strain on these sites. Certain locations, such as Dovedale in the Peak District are especially popular and are known as 'honeypot attractions', because of the way visitors flock to them as bees would around a honeypot. Honeypot attractions sometimes suffer from excessive visitor numbers, which in turn can lead to road congestion, localised air pollution, footpath erosion and disruption to local communities. There is a delicate balance between encouraging visitors and protecting the environments they come to enjoy. With tourism and car use both increasing, the challenge is likely to become even greater in the future.

Heath and moorlands are among the UK's threatened environments that are protected by national parks.

UK NATIONAL PARKS

CAIRNGORMS	3,800km^2
LAKE DISTRICT	2,292km^2
SNOWDONIA (ERYRI)	2,142km^2
LOCH LOMOND AND THE TROSSACHS	1,865km^2
YORKSHIRE DALES	1,769km^2
THE PEAK DISTRICT	1,438km^2
NORTH YORK MOORS	1,432km^2
BRECON BEACONS	1,351km^2
NORTHUMBERLAND	1,049km^2
DARTMOOR	954km^2
EXMOOR	693km^2
PEMBROKESHIRE COAST	620km^2
THE BROADS	303km^2

Source: The Association of National Park Authorities

This statue shows Birmingham's transition from its industrial past into the modern era. The leading figure represents Maurice Wilkins, a Birmingham-trained scientist who won the Nobel Prize for his work on DNA.

CONTINUED REFORMS

The UK will undergo continued reforms in the early part of the twenty-first century as it completes the modernisation of its economy. Industry will continue to decline except for the specialised manufacture of hi-tech products and components. In contrast, the service sector will continue to expand, particularly in the leisure industry. Agriculture in the UK will become even less significant following the succession of food scares and diseases that have plagued the sector in recent years. The exception to this pattern will be organic farming, which is expected to expand to meet the annual doubling in demand for organic produce, 70 per cent of which is currently imported rather than produced locally. Continued reforms will also be seen in transport and energy, both of which will have to adopt more sustainable approaches if the UK is to meet its various environmental commitments.

In terms of social policy, the main challenges facing the UK are to revive the NHS, and to ensure that everyone in the UK has equal opportunities for high-quality education and the chance to learn the skills necessary for finding employment. This will require special effort in the more deprived areas of the UK that have suffered more than most as industries have closed, scaled down or relocated. The UK will become more ethnically diverse in the future, especially if immigration is encouraged to supply the shortfall of labour expected as a result of an ageing population. Such patterns are already evident, with nurses being recruited from the Philippines in 2000–2001 to fill staff shortages in the NHS. Whilst such diversity should be beneficial to the UK, recent experiences suggest that ethnic differences can be exaggerated into local conflicts, often hiding wider problems such as unemployment, poverty or crime. In the summer of 2001 ethnic conflicts became violent and resulted in damage to both people and property in several UK cities.

INTO EUROPE?

The biggest change to affect the UK in the coming years will be its decision on whether or not to adopt the Euro and extend its links with Europe to monetary union. Opinion is divided at present as to the benefits of the UK joining the so-called 'Euro-zone'. Those who support the Euro claim it would simplify and encourage trade, benefiting UK companies. Critics believe that the UK would become too reliant on Europe, and lose its international reputation and independence. For the British public, the biggest concern seems to be the loss of the British pound as a currency. In fact feelings are so strong that in the 2001 General Election several political parties stood for election purely on the basis of saving the

A political wall painting in Northern Ireland. The fragile negotiations between opposing groups in Northern Ireland will hopefully bring lasting peace.

The London Eye provides a spectacular platform from which to view the changing landscape of London as it leads the UK into the twenty-first century.

pound. The final decision will be down to the UK people themselves, as the government has promised a referendum allowing them to vote whether or not to join the Euro-zone. The outcome will play a major role in determining the future of the UK. However, since it is less than 100 years since the British ruled over nearly half the world's population and barely 50 years since the end of the last war, the UK is used to change.

GLOSSARY

Arable farming A farming system that focuses on growing plant crops, normally grains such as wheat, maize and barley, among others.

Basalt A black or dark grey rock formed as a result of cooled molten magma from volcanic activity. Basalt can cool and solidify into hexagonal columns such as those in the Giant's Causeway.

Biodegradable A substance that can be broken down and recycled by naturally occurring organisms.

Biofuels A term used to describe fuels made up of biological material such as timber or methane gas, which is generated as biological matter decomposes.

Colonisation The process whereby one country takes political control of another.

Devolution A process in which part of a country is given greater control of its own affairs and the central government becomes less involved (devolved).

Euro ( ) The new common currency used in EMU countries and replacing their old currencies as of January 2002. The UK has so far resisted joining the EMU and so keeps the pound (sterling).

European Monetary Union (EMU) A group of European nations who have agreed to share a common European currency (the Euro –   ) and dispose of their own currencies. The EMU should improve trade between member countries.

Global economy Trade and businesses are increasingly operating at a global level thanks to modern communications. Such transactions are said to take place in the global economy.

Grey vote As populations age, elderly people (who often have grey hair) become a larger proportion of the total population and so have a bigger influence on governments by the way they vote.

Gross Domestic Product (GDP) The monetary value of goods and services produced by a country in a single year.

Gross National Income (GNI) The monetary value of the goods and services produced by a country plus any earnings from overseas in a single year.

Hydroelectric power (HEP) Electricity generated by water as it passes through turbines. These normally involve large dams across river valleys that form artificial lakes behind them.

Integrated transport systems Systems in which different forms of transport, such as buses, trains, trams and cars, are co-ordinated to improve people's mobility and reduce pollution pressure on the environment.

Landfill sites Holes or hollows in the ground used for burying waste from human activities. Once full they are covered over and the land is often used for building or leisure activities.

Leachate A liquid formed when water enters a landfill site and carries diluted chemicals and metals with it as it passes through the rubbish. Leachate can pollute local water resources.

Megawatt (MW) A measure of electrical power most often used to describe the power output of electricity sources such as power stations or wind farms (1 MW is equal to 1 million Watts).

Multiplier effect The process whereby one event leads to another. Sometimes known as a 'domino effect' or 'knock-on effect'. This process can be positive or negative and is often used in economics.

National Assembly A group of elected individuals who have a responsibility for governing their people (the nation).

Nationalisation The process of making an organisation or industry the property of the nation as opposed to the property of individuals.

'Out-of-town' economy The pattern whereby large sections of the economy such as businesses, industry, retail stores and leisure facilities move to locations outside main towns, often on specially constructed sites.

Privatisation The process whereby a national property is sold to individuals to become privately owned and managed.

Referendum Allowing members of the public to vote on a major issue. The UK is likely to have a referendum about joining the EMU.

Renewable energy Energy from sources that are continually available, such the wind or the sun. Non-renewable sources include coal, oil and gas – once used, they cannot be used again.

Set-aside An agricultural practice where land is left fallow because it is not needed to produce food or is left to protect the environment. Farmers are normally paid by the government for leaving this land fallow.

Social exclusion When an individual or group of people is isolated from the broader society in which they live.

Sustainable development Development that meets the needs of today without compromising the ability of future generations to meet their needs.

'Teletubby generation' The term used to describe the increasingly overweight child population in the UK.

Toxic Organic Micro Pollutants (TOMPs) A group of pollutants produced by the incomplete burning of fuels or waste. TOMPs are highly toxic, even in small quantities, and some are carcinogenic (believed to cause cancer).

Transport hubs Key points (hubs) where different modes of transport meet. Roads may meet with a railway terminal or port for example, allowing the easy transfer of goods.

Veggie-box schemes Schemes whereby local farm produce is delivered direct from the farms to nearby communities, reducing the need for transportation over long distances.

Welfare State A system of public services and benefits provided by the government and set up in 1948. They include free healthcare under the National Health Service (NHS).

Wind farm A series of wind turbines generating electricity for the national electricity network.

FURTHER INFORMATION

BOOKS TO READ:

Country Fact Files: the United Kingdom by David Flint (Hodder Wayland, 1998). Illustrated reference for KS3.

Exploring Geography Book 1: The UK and the Local Environment by Simon Ross and Peter Eyre (Longman, 1991). Textbook for KS3 looking at the UK and the local environment.

Exploring Geography Book 2: The UK Within Europe by Ann Beckwith and Anne Sutcliffe (Longman, 1991). Textbook for KS3 looking at the UK's relationship with Europe.

Geographical Case Studies: The United Kingdom by Chris Burnett, Keith Flinders and Barnaby Lenon (Hodder & Stoughton Educational, 1995). A case study based text on the UK for KS3–4.

The Rough Guide To Britain by Robert Andrews and others (Rough Guides, 2004). An informative travel guide to Britain though it excludes Northern Ireland.

WEBSITES:

GENERAL INFORMATION
http://msn.expedia.com/wg/Europe/United_Kingdom/P2796.asp/
A good general knowledge and enquiry site to find out more about the UK.

PEOPLE
http://www.royal.gov.uk/
The official website of the British Monarchy.

ENVIRONMENT
http://www.anpa.gov.uk/
Website for The Association of National Park Authorities (ANPA) with information and links to all the UK's national parks.

http://www.doingyourbit.org.uk/
UK government website (from the Department of Environment, Food and Rural Affairs) promoting greater environmental awareness.

http://www.cat.org.uk/
The Centre for Alternative Technology in Machynlleth, Wales, provides information about sustainable development and how to get involved.

PLACES
http://www.aboutbritain.com/
Useful entry website allowing you to search for more about the UK's regions, towns and attractions.

TOURISM
http://www.enjoybritain.com/
A website offering links for everything to do with travel and tourism in the UK.

http://www.visitbritain.com/
The official visitors site for the British Tourist Authority – a useful virtual tour in 'Images of Britain'.

INDEX

Numbers shown in **bold** also refer to pages with maps, graphic illustrations or photographs.

The famous Lloyds building, designed by Richard Rogers, is a dramatic feature of the London skyline.

Sheep graze on rolling green farmland